Memories of a Lifetime™

Fairies & Angels

ARTWORK FOR SCRAPBOOKS AND FABRIC-TRANSFER CRAFTS

Nancy Rosin

Sterling Publishing Co., Inc. New York
A Sterling/Chapelle Book

Author: Nancy Rosin

If you have any questions or comments, please contact:
Chapelle, Ltd., Inc., P.O. Box 9252, Ogden, UT 84409
(801) 621-2777 • (801) 621-2788 Fax
e-mail: chapelle@chapelleltd.com
Web site: www.chapelleltd.com

PC Configuration: Windows 98 or later with 128 MB Ram or greater. At least 100 MB of free hard disc space. Dual speed or faster CD-ROM drive, and a 24-bit color monitor.

Macintosh Configuration: Mac OS 9 or later with 128 MB Ram or greater. At least 100 MB of free hard disk space. Dual speed or faster CD-ROM drive, and a 24-bit color monitor.

10 9 8 7 6 5 4 3 2

Published by Sterling Publishing Co., Inc.
387 Park Avenue South, New York, NY 10016
© 2005 by Sterling Publishing Co., Inc.
Distributed in Canada by Sterling Publishing
c/o Canadian Manda Group, 165 Dufferin Street
Toronto, Ontario, Canada M6K 3H6
Distributed in Great Britain by Chrysalis Books Group PLC,
The Chrysalis Building, Bramley Road, London W10 6SP, England
Distributed in Australia by Capricorn Link (Australia) Pty. Ltd.
P. O. Box 704, Windsor, NSW 2756, Australia
Printed and Bound in China
All Rights Reserved

Sterling ISBN 1-4027-2640-6

For information about custom editions, special sales, premium and corporate purchases, please contact Sterling Special Sales Department at 800-805-5489 or specialsales@sterlingpub.com.

InTroducTion

Imagine having hundreds of rare, vintage images right at your fingertips. With our *Memories of a Lifetime*™ series, that's exactly what you get. We've scoured antique stores, estate sales, and other outlets to find one-of-a-kind images to give your projects the flair that only old-time artwork can provide. From Victorian postcards to hand-painted beautiful borders and frames, it would take years to acquire a collection like this. However, with this easy-to-use resource, you'll have them all—right here, right now.

Each image has been reproduced to the highest quality standard for photocopying and scanning; reduce or enlarge them to suit your needs. A CD-Rom containing all of the images in digital form is included, enabling you to use them for any computer project over and again. If you prefer to use them as they're printed, simply cut them out—they're printed on one side only.

Perfect for paper crafting, scrapbooking, and fabric transfers, *Memories of a Lifetime*™ books will inspire you to explore new avenues of creativity. We've included a sampling of ideas to get you started, but the best part is using your imagination to create your own fabulous projects. Be sure to look for other books in this series as we continue to search the markets for wonderful vintage images.

How to Use This Book

General Instructions:

These images are printed on one side only, making it easy to simply cut out the desired image. However, you'll probably want to use them again, so we have included a CD-Rom which contains all of the images individually as well as in the page layout form. The CDs can be used with both PC and Mac formats. Just pop in the disk. On a PC, the file will immediately open to the Home page, which will walk you through how to view and print the images. For Macintosh® users, you will simply double-click on the icon to open. The images may also be incorporated into your computer projects using simple imaging software that you can purchase specifically for this purpose—a perfect choice for digital scrapbooking.

The reference numbers printed on the back of each image in the book are the same ones used on the CD, which will allow you to easily find the image you are looking for. The numbering consists of the book abbreviation, the page number, the image number, and the file format. The first file number (located next to the page number) is for the entire page. For example, FA01-001.jpg would be the entire image for page 1 of *Fairies & Angels*. The second file number is for the top-right image. The numbers continue in a counterclockwise fashion.

Once you have resized your images, added text, created a scrapbook page, etc., you are ready to print them out. Printing on cream or white cardstock, particularly a textured variety, creates a more authentic look. You won't be able to tell that it's a reproduction! If you don't have access to a computer or printer, that's ok. Most photocopy centers can resize and print your images for a nominal fee, or they have do-it-yourself machines that are easy to use.

Ideas for Using the Images:

Scrapbooking: These images are perfect for both heritage and modern scrapbook pages. Simply use the image as a frame, accent piece, or border. For those of you with limited time, the page layouts in this book have been created so that you can use them as they are. Simply print out or photocopy the desired page, attach a photograph into one of the boxes, and you have a beautiful scrapbook page in minutes. For a little dimension, add a ribbon or charm. Be sure to print your images onto acid-free card-stock so the pages will last a lifetime.

Cards: Some computer programs allow images to be inserted into a card template, simplifying cardmaking. If this is not an option, simply use the images as accent pieces on the front or inside of the card. Use a bone folder to score the card's fold to create a more professional look.

Decoupage/Collage Projects: For decoupage or collage projects, photocopy or print the image onto a thinner paper such as copier paper. Thin paper adheres to projects more effectively. Decoupage medium glues and seals the project, creating a gloss or matte finish when dry, thus protecting the image. Vintage images are beautiful when decoupaged to cigar boxes, glass plates, and even wooden plaques. The possibilities are endless.

Fabric Arts: Vintage images can be used in just about any fabric craft imaginable: wall hangings, quilts, bags, or baby bibs. Either transfer the image onto the fabric by using a special iron-on paper, or by printing the image directly onto the fabric, using a temporary iron-on stabilizer that stabilizes the fabric to feed through a printer. These items are available at most craft and sewing stores. If the item will be washed, it is better to print directly on the fabric. For either method, follow the instructions on the package.

Wood Transfers: It is now possible to "print" images on wood. Use this exciting technique to create vintage plaques, clocks, frames, and more. A simple, inexpensive transfer tool is available at most large craft or home improvement stores, or online from various manufacturers. You simply place the photocopy of the image you want, face down, onto the surface and use the tool to transfer the image onto the wood. This process requires a copy from a laser printer, which means you will probably have to get your copies made at a copy center. Refer to manufacturer's instructions for additional details. There are other transfer products available that can be used with wood. Choose the one that is easiest for you.

Gallery of Ideas

These images can be used in a variety of projects: cards, scrapbook pages, and decoupage projects to name a few. The images can be used as they are shown in the layout, or you can copy and clip out individual images, or even portions or multitudes of images. The following pages contain a collection of ideas to inspire you to use your imagination and create one-of-a-kind treasures.

Special Angel

Rachel Christine

~ September 19, 2004 ~

You are my special angel, sent from up above.

This layout demonstrates how you can take individual elements of a favorite art page, copy and resize the elements as desired, and create your own unique page in very little time.

Because the images supplied on the CD can be sized as desired, it is easy to create the proper frame size for your perfect photo. Elements can also be duplicated to give you just the look you want, as we have done here by running the daisy border across both the top and bottom of the page.

A Love to Share

Special sisters, special friends, special angels. "May you always watch out for each other."

The small layouts above and below show how some of the images actually appear on the art pages of this book. The scrapbook page at right is an example of taking any of the images that appeal to you, and creating a beautiful, one-of-a-kind page. This is a wonderful way to create spreads that will be visually appealing when placed side-by-side in your photo album.

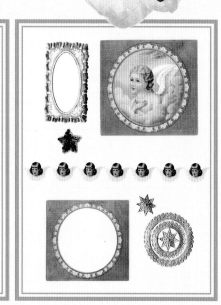

A Wonderful
Winter

Sparkling Snow Angel

To make this fanciful holiday decoration, enlarge one of your favorite angel images and print it out on cardstock. Add a touch of dimension by attaching a delicate ribbon and gluing some tiny paper flowers into the basket. A small paper easel can be attached to the back so that your angel can stand.

To add the "sparkle," use a paintbrush to paint a thin layer of paper glue to areas you wish to embellish. Sprinkle on German glass glitter. This type of glitter will patina gradually, giving your project a beautiful antique finish over time.

What fabulous cards
you can create, using
some of the fun images
in this book! These
fairy divas where given
that extra flair by
adding a feather to
their headdresses.

Images can be either printed
directly onto cardstock or cut out
and attached to the front
of a card blank. If you choose
to make your own cards, be
certain to use a bone folder
to create a crisp fold and a
professional finish.

Fairy Cards

Cheerful Tote

Fabric transferring is a wonderful way to use vintage images. You can create quilt blocks, add images to handbags, personalize T-shirts—the ideas are endless. Fabric transfer sheets are readily available in craft and office supply stores. Remember to always follow manufacturer's instructions because there are different types of this product on the market.

This plain paiper-mâché star-shaped box was turned into "wow" by using a little glitter, glue, and some fabulous vintage images.

Star Box

Use a paintbrush to spread a thin layer of glue around the sides of the box and lid. Sprinkle with colored glitter and let dry for several hours. Decoupage the top of the lid with the desired images. Trim the top of the lid with a contrasting color of glitter.

A metallic photo mat was used to frame this angelic image. Ribbon and cord create a nice border. This beautiful work of art can be used as a greeting card or framed to enjoy for years to come.

Victorian Card

FA01-003   FA01-002

FA01-004   FA01-006

                    FA01-005

1— FA01-001

FA02-003

FA02-002

FA02-004

FA02-005   FA02-010   FA02-009   FA02-008

FA02-006

FA02-007

FA02-001   2

FA03-003   FA03-002

FA03-004   FA03-007

FA03-005   FA03-006

3 — FA03-001

FA04-004

FA04-002

FA04-003

FA04-008

FA04-005

FA04-007

FA04-006

FA04-001 — 4

FA05-004   FA05-002

                    FA05-003

                    FA05-005

                    FA05-006   FA05-008

FA05-007

5 — FA05-001

FA06-004   FA06-003   FA06-002

                                          FA06-008

FA06-005

FA06-006   FA06-007

FA07-003   FA07-002

FA07-004   FA07-008

FA07-005   FA07-007

FA07-006

7 ─ FA07-001

FA08-003

FA08-002

FA08-007

FA08-004

FA08-006

FA08-005

FA08-001

Our Own
LITTLE
FAIRY'S
BATH
PERFUME

LINCOLN CHEMICAL WORKS
CHICAGO, ILL.

SIX
PICTURE
PUZZLES
Series No. 422
Made by
MADMAR QUALITY CO.
UTICA, N.Y.

Ruth Eger

COMPLIMENTS OF THE SEASON
JULIUS SAUL.
SPRING 1884

FA09-003   FA09-002

FA09-004   FA09-007   FA09-006

FA09-001   FA09-005

FA10-002

FA10-009

FA10-008

FA10-003

FA10-007

FA10-006

FA10-005

FA10-004

FA10-001 10

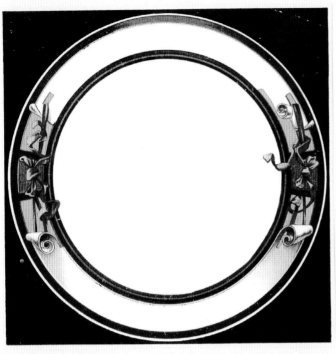

KNAPP'S THROAT CURE (Lozenge.)
FOR THROAT & VOICE.

Price 25 cents

"A godsend to vocalists, invaluable in emergencies"
SIG. ERRANI New York.
"Its curative properties are simply wonderful"
Rev. H. W. KNAPP, D.D. N.Y.
SEE THE HISTORY OF A VOICE LOST AND WON, OR ADDRESS
EDWARD A. OLDS, 100 Fulton St New York   Box 2985

FA11-003   FA11-002

FA11-004

FA11-005   FA11-006

FA11-001

FA12-003

FA12-002

FA12-004

FA12-005

FA12-006

FA12-001

12

FA13-003   FA13-002

FA13-004   FA13-005

FA14-003

FA14-002

FA14-004

FA14-005

FA14-006

ГА14-007   ГА14-016   ГА14-015   ГА14-012

FA14-014

FA14-008

FA14-013

FA14-009   FA14-010   FA14-011

L'Ange Gardien

Les Bonnes Fées

LA FÉE
ESPÉRANCE

Joyeuses Pâques

L'Ange de la Patrie

Prions bien tous les deux pour notre cher Papa
Le bon ange gardien nous le protégera

RÉPUBLIQUE FRANÇAISE
5c
POSTES

RÉPUBLIQUE FRANÇAISE
5c
POSTES

DIX
1484

Bonne
Année

E. L. D.

FA15-004

FA15-003

FA15-002

FA15-008

FA15-005

FA15-007

FA15-006

15 — FA15-001

FA16-003

FA16-004

FA16-002

FA16-005

FA16-006

FA16-007

FA16-008

FA16-012

FA16-009

FA16-010

FA16-011

HALL'S
VEGETABLE SICILIAN
HAIR RENEWER
Prevents gray hairs and baldness

OVER

FA17-003   FA17-002

FA17-004   FA17-007

FA17-005   FA17-006

FA17-001

FA18-003   FA18-002

FA18-004

FA18-005   FA18-006

FA19-004   FA19-003   FA19-002

FA19-005

FA19-006   FA19-007

FA19-001

FA20-003   FA20-002

FA20-004   FA20-005

FA20-001 — 20

Heureuses Pâques

FA21-003   FA21-002

                                           FA21-007

FA21-004   FA21-009   FA21-008

        FA21-005   FA21-006

FA22-003   FA22-002

FA22-004   FA22-005

                                        FA22-009   FA22-008

FA22-006   FA22-007

FA23-003   FA23-002

                                                        FA23-007

              FA23-004   FA23-005

                                                        FA23-006

23 ─┤ FA23-001 │

FA24-003   FA24-002

FA24-004   FA24-005

FA25-003   FA25-002

FA25-004   FA25-006

FA25-005

FA25-001

FA26-003

FA26-002

FA26-004

FA26-006

FA26-005

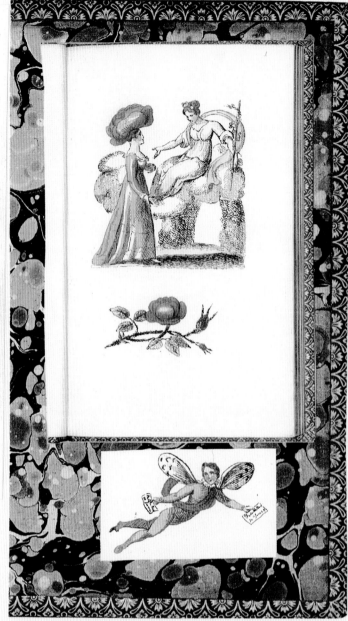

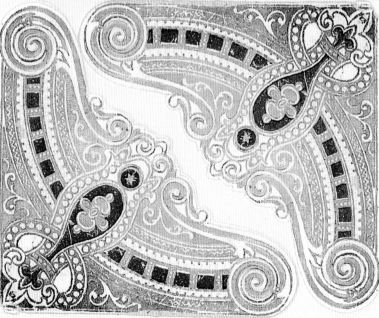

In Summer may your happy hours
Be numerous as the Summer flowers

May all the joys that Hope can bring
Be yours, like blossoms in the Spring

May Autumn's plenty fill your store
And want ne'er enter at your door

In Winter may your fireside be
The home of mirth and jollity.

FA27-004

FA27-006

FA27-005

FA27-003

FA27-002

FA27-007

FA27-008

FA27-009

27 — FA27-001

FA28-003

FA28-002

FA28-006

FA28-004

FA28-005

VÉRITABLE EXTRAIT DE VIANDE LIEBIG.

LES SYLPHIDES.
Ronde au clair de lune.

Voir au verso.

HE LOVES ME A LITTLE

FA29-003   FA29-002

                        FA29-004

                              FA29-008   FA29-007

        FA29-005   FA29-006

FA30-003   FA30-002

FA30-004

FA30-005

FA31-002

FA31-003

FA31-007

FA31-004

FA31-006

FA31-005

FA31-001

FA32-003

FA32-002

FA32-004   FA32-005

FA32-006

FA32-007   FA32-008

FA32-009

FA32-010

FA32-001 32

Wild Duck. 18   Swan.

Flamingo.

Demoiselle
Crane.   Marabu.

O BIRDIE, pray lead us
Straight home to your nest,
And show us your nestlings,
And which you love best:

And show us some fairies,
Asleep in their flowers,
Or under the mushrooms,
In deep mossy bowers;

While the breeze and the sunshine
Hide and seek through the boughs,
We'll plight on the green sward
Our love and our vows.

YOU TELL ME LITTLE TALES
Of fairy and of elf
But I would rather hear
you talk
About your little self
THE FAIRY QUEEN goes by, you say
Drawn in a lily car
Believe me you are twice as fair
And sweeter too by far

FA33-003   FA33-002

FA33-004

                                      FA33-007

FA33-005   FA33-006

FA34-003   FA34-002

FA34-004

FA34-005   FA34-008

                    FA34-006   FA34-007

FA34-001 34

FA35-003   FA35-002

                        FA35-007

                                      FA35-006

                                      FA35-005

FA35-004

FA35-001

FA36-002

FA36-003

FA37-003

FA37-002

FA37-007

FA37-006

FA37-004

FA37-005

FA37-001

FA38-003

FA38-002

FA38-004

FA38-005

DAINTY AIRS (continued.)

And the ... ren ... an-sw ... men and wo - men:- Such a pret-ty play!"

Ah, dear lit-tle ... ain would be like you!

Bear my friend my gree - ting, ... be as hap - py As we are to - day."

Words by G. P. Meade.　　　　MARCUS WARD & CO.　　　　Music by B. Hobson Carroll.

FA39-002

FA39-003   FA39-004

FA40-003   FA40-002

FA40-004   FA40-011   FA40-010   FA40-009

        FA40-005

        FA40-006

        FA40-007   FA40-008

VÉRITABLE EXTRAIT DE VIANDE LIEBIG.

LES SYLPHIDES.
Hors d'ici, intrus!

Voir au verso.

VÉRITABLE EXTRAIT DE VIANDE LIEBIG.

LES SYLPHIDES.
La balançoire fleurie.

Voir au verso.

VÉRITABLE EXTRAIT DE VIANDE LIEBIG.

LES SYLPHIDES.
La danse aux papillons.

Voir au verso.

FA41-004

FA41-003   FA41-002

FA41-005   FA41-011

FA41-012

FA41-006   FA41-010

FA41-007   FA41-008

FA41-009

FA42-003

FA42-002

FA42-004   FA42-005   FA42-006

Merry Christmas

FA43-003   FA43-002

FA43-004   FA43-005

FA44-003   FA44-002

                                              FA44-008

FA44-004   FA44-009

FA44-005   FA44-006

                                              FA44-007

EASTER
Blessing.

Holy
be
thy
EASTER.

A
Holy
EASTER.

May Tender
many blessings
rest

Upon this
Easter
Day.

FA45-003   FA45-002

FA45-004   FA45-005

FA45-001

FA46-003   FA46-002

                        FA46-004

FA46-005   FA46-006

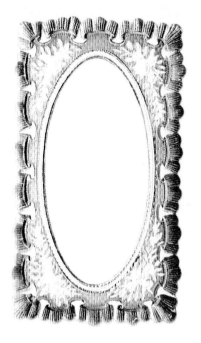

FA47-003   FA47-002

                                                FA47-008

                    FA47-004

            FA47-005

    FA47-006   FA47-007

FA47-001

FA48-003   FA48-002

FA48-004   FA48-005

FA48-001   48

Were I The Fairy-
God-Mother
Who came to bless your birth,
Instead of granting wishes Three,
I'd give you All The
Earth!

MESSENGER OF LOVE.

FA49-003

FA49-002

FA49-004

FA49-007

FA49-005

FA49-006

FA49-001

FA50-003

FA50-002

FA50-006

FA50-004

FA50-005

FA50-001 50

FA51-003   FA51-002

FA51-004

FA51-005   FA51-007

FA51-006

FA52-003   FA52-002

                  FA52-004

FA52-005   FA52-008

FA52-006   FA52-007

I love you.

FA53-003　　　　　　　　　　　　　FA53-002

　　　　　　　　　　　　　　　　　　　　FA53-008

FA53-004

　　　　　　　　　　　　　FA53-007

FA53-005　　　　　FA53-006

FA54-003

FA54-002

FA54-004

FA54-005

FA54-001

FROM ONE WHO LOVES YOU DEARLY.

FA55-002

FA55-003   FA55-006

FA55-004   FA55-005

FA56-002

FA56-003

FA56-006

FA56-004

FA56-005

FA56-001 56

FA57-003

FA57-002

FA57-004   FA57-005

FA57-001